HOW TO SURVIVE THE OFFICE

The ultimate guide

Jeremy Young

I am dying from the treatment of too many physicians

ALEXANDER THE GREAT

CONTENTS

PREFACE

After I turned 40, I started to feel uncomfortably numb at the office. I was not getting the satisfaction I used to get from work. Every task, every meeting, every new project started to look the same to me.

There are tons of books on the world of business. Subjects range from how to find a job, how to manage meetings, how to be a C.E.O., how to balance work and life... And do not even get me started on the unending pieces of training on professional development. None seemed to provide *practical* solutions that applied to daily office life.

As Alexander the Great said, "I am dying from the treatment of too many physicians", I started to feel almost sick after going through all these business books, coaching, and training.

I decided to write this book to share my honest thoughts about common subjects of office life. As someone who has worked for numerous, public, private, family-owned American, European, Middle Eastern, and Asian businesses across many different countries, in the last 20 years, I have seen the insides of more offices than I prefer to count.

Despite the variety of jobs and employers I have worked for, the similarities of office life all over the world are striking. The problems experienced by junior associates, executive staff, and C.E.O.s, though at different levels of complexity, are remarkably alike. Equally similar are the promoted solutions in M.B.A. degrees, associated business books, and soft skills development training programs. What do they have in common? They do not work. Why? Because they do not tackle the core issue.

The awakening for me came in 2016 as I was trying to get used to my new role in an unfamiliar country. I started feeling a lot of stress. In my search for someone to help, I came across a Shaman who taught me a simple lesson. He told me that I was killing myself, trying to make everything perfect when perfection is never truly possible. The cherry on the cake was that I kept blaming myself for existing problems in my new company, none of which had anything to do with me. His advice?

"Get some paint and a large canvas and paint with your bare hands to relax and clear your mind."

Life will become less complicated when we accept the dynamics of office life as is. I learned this through trial and error. Through this book, I hope to save you from these trials and tribulations and guide you as my Shaman did for me. You will learn how to compartmentalize your life through the insights gained through this book and enjoy your limited time on this planet.

To start, wake up and look at your life in the office from a realistic lens. Here is where classical and contemporary business literature fails. I hope to convey to you that this book will most probably not inspire you in the beginning.

Instead, I aspire to show you the honest reality of office life, how to develop acceptance, how to find happiness in that acceptance, and how to build a life away from the frenzy of work - life is more than just your job. I hope the book will inspire you to do just that.

INTRODUCTION

The problem with today's business books is that they try to paint an idealistic picture where none exists in the real world. All these 'suggestions' are based on this false premise. Hence, most solutions to office problems are superficial at best and severely damaging at the worst. As Albert Einstein said, "We can't solve problems by using the same thinking we used when we created them."

Modern business literature available currently ignores the anthropologic fact that current employment contracts evolved from the slavery of human beings, replacing food and shelter for labor with employee benefits for work. However, the basic premise remains. He/she who pays your salary has the last word. Their ego and power are only restrained by ethics & personal values (if it exists) and employment law. Those could be nonexistent, insufficient, or well ignored, as seen in the Harvey

Weinstein case, that took place in one of the most democratic countries in the world, where the law is supposedly above everyone. Imagine if this can happen in America, what would the plight of the rest of the world be. It took so long for the transgressions to come up to surface.

I have seen a significant number of professionals, office workers at different career levels, having severe anxieties bordering on dangerous psychological problems that persist not only professionally, but also in their personal lives.

I knew of an executive assistant who used to mix Bailey's with her Starbucks coffee after every lunch. I asked her why, and she answered, "This is the only way I can survive this guy," this guy referring to our boss at the time.

I worked with a senior executive with severe alcohol issues because of the constant nerve-wracking pressure from the company's shareholders. He used to receive calls at eleven-thirty at night, asking for supplier contractual details so extreme, that no human being can come up with at an instant.

I, too, have personally felt similar impacts in my life. Looking back, I ask myself, why did I allow myself to be so coerced? Did I end up inventing anything? Did I discover the cure for cancer? Did anyone around me do one of these? No, I just made my fair contribution to the business society in several continents and different cultures. I got paid my share (whether fair or not is up for debate, but it was a mutually agreed amount). As per senior leaders and shareholders, who were my bosses, they have received their fair share of returns. Well, at least I am convinced they did, much more than they had initially expected. To be honest, only they would be able to answer this accurately.

So why the stress? Why the drama? Yet there is still so much of this commotion in the workplace. Most, if not all, of it, can be avoided.

To be fair, there are things you can do yourself and things you cannot control. That is where the stoic approach falls in to play. Like the famous Stoic Marcus Aurelius, expect the worst, accept whatever comes. Remember that life is more substantial than what you experience every day at work. This book tries to show you the worst that can happen in the office so that it will be easier for you to accept your circumstances in full, whatever they may be.

A small disclaimer: in no way would I like to argue that offices are full of mean-spirited psychopaths. But I am sure any office worker can name a few co-workers who would be better off institutionalized.

Unfortunately, I have experienced firsthand that to be prepared in a mental state expecting this will be much better for you than believing the M.B.A. stuff peddled in modern business literature and forcing yourself to be the office Pollyanna.

Keeping your expectations from the office to a minimum almost guarantees your happiness and health. You might ask yourself, what is the cost of this approach. There are no free lunches in the corporate world. Taking this approach might have consequences, and you might be giving up on some career opportunities. If you do not play by the rules, you will probably not be offered or granted higher positions in your career. That is a choice you have to make. If you play by the rules, you will bear the cost, as you will read in the following chapters. If you chose to take a wiser approach, the one I recommend, you would achieve the upside of a more holistic approach to life. You will have the time to work on stuff that you are really passionate about, and not the tasks dictated to you by your employer's corporate vision or mission statement.

In this respect, I am launching an initiative with www.HowToSurviveTheOffice.com to remind you of the facts of office life and for you to share your work and office stories anonymously. I will be contributing advice to your particular problems and hope to maintain a platform to show you that you are not the only one in this rat race. Suppose you can free yourself and understand the fundamental premise that the office is where you rent out your hours and get paid for it. In that case, it will be easier for you to find acceptance.

The book starts with Chapter 1: "Get Hired!". While painting a realistic picture of the players in the game like human resources and recruiters, this chapter provides guidance for you to efficiently navigate any hurdles. Your life in this new job that you are about to get is mostly, if not entirely, influenced by how you manage your recruitment and associated negotiation process.

Then comes chapter 2 with "Make an awesome entry" Without giving away too much, this chapter is a fun read!

Chapter 3 "Know Your Boundaries" and Chapter 4, "Do you think you can survive without a fight?" explain how to protect yourself from unnecessary conflict. Almost all conflict is avoidable. You will understand the fundamental strategies to handle them if they occur, while also learning how to identify them before they arise.

Chapter 5: "Common Traps" defines the booby traps that exist in every company. I have seen C.E.O.s, directors, and interns stepping on them and losing their metaphorical legs. If you do not know how to recognize the traps, it will be only a matter of time before you get caught in one.

Chapter 6 "Winter is coming" and Chapter 7 "Should I stay, or should I go?" explain the inevitable end of your tenure in the company and include valuable recommendations to make it a smoother process.

If you have lost your job or fired your boss, jump to chapter 8, "Tears dry on their own" and read along. You will feel better as you understand that this is where we all are going to end up in any way.

GET HIRED!

There are multiple ways to approach your search for a job. Let us first discuss online platforms. While job websites like LinkedIn, Monster, etc. are flourishing, it also points to the fact that recruiters have increasingly simsimilar-looking, inflated resumes on their desks!

Be incredibly careful about how much time you dedicate to those platforms in your search for a job- it is deceivingly easy to get lost in them. Be careful! Remember, there are tons of people like you applying to these positions, and much like a casino, only the house wins. Do not forget that these platforms are mainly social networks, and their main aim is to capture your attention and get you hooked on the platform, not to get you a job!

One way to use these social platforms to apply for

a job is to look for advertisements where the recruiter leaves a phone number to discuss the role. Do not hesitate to call that number. Such recruiters are usually very friendly. They add a phone number for you to call them because they are probably desperate to fill the role. Be proactive and get in touch!

A word of caution while communication with recruiters- do not stalk them! Recruiters are like real estate brokers; they make good money on a sale or successful recruitment. They will pursue you if they believe you are the right candidate. Once you have sent in an introduction and a resume, wait. Yes, wait. No, do not press "send" on that follow-up mail. No, do not text them asking for the status of your application. No, no, no, and one more time for good measure, NO!

The recruiter's probability of forgetting you if you are the perfect candidate for the job is close to ZERO. Most likely, if you repeatedly follow up, your ambition will be misunderstood as desperation. In case the recruiter has a relevant opening in the future, you will start that discussion with a psychological disadvantage. Not ideal!

When the recruiter reaches out to you, be responsive. However, be careful that the information shared is beneficial to you. For example, never provide your base salary, only what you expect. Your base salary is your biggest negotiation lever. Do not, in any conversation, provide this data. I am not saying that you should lie. However, it is a golden rule that your current compensation is confidential information and should remain between you and your current or last employer. That information is probably under a confidentiality clause somewhere in your employment contract or general law. Why would you voluntarily break your contractual obligations to your detriment? Yet, I admit that this is a mistake I have committed many times, for which I paid handsomely. We make this mistake because some recruiters are particularly good at causing us emotional stress during the interview, making us feel that the recruitment process will not proceed in the absence of this information. The information you need to provide at this stage is your expected salary and your willingness to negotiate. Full stop.

The other way of finding a job is to know someone in a position of authority in the company who could arrange a job interview. The dynamics of that meeting are vastly different, and that is what we will discuss now.

There are two ways such introductions could go. The first scenario is that there is a vacancy, and you know someone who knows someone with authority to hire for that position. You have got your lucky break! Be prepared, dress well, and do not mess it up. Period.

The second case is that the company does not have an advertised vacancy. You happen to meet someone with high authority in the company. That someone could be the C.E.O., board member, key advisor, owner, etc. This is where it gets exciting! Every company needs qualified and motivated new staff. This is your chance to score that undefined, unadvertised vacancy. For this to work, you must be able to sell your value to the company. Do not forget, a position will not be created for you because you are a lovely human being, but only if you manage to create a communicational synergy and convince them that your presence adds immense value to the organization.

Apart from my first, all other jobs I found, or I was found for, were through my network. Lately, in my career, I have come to accept the conclusion that my superiors in the company, be it the C.E.O., board, or even shareholders, may not be qualified to the extend everyone gives them credit for. Large amounts of power and wealth are transferred nowadays through inheritance or on the display of loyalty for an extended period, and not necessarily merit.

I have also experienced firsthand that job brokers or headhunters usually have only one goal: to close the position and invoice the customer for their retainer fee. They are inclined to present you for jobs that are not in your best interest and are happy to fake a rosy picture of the candidate (to the employer) and the company (to the candidate) to finalize their assignment.

I have come to realize that most of the recruitment process is finalized before your interview. However, if you happen to enter this round with a weak hand, it will be challenging to turn it around in the meeting.

I have to say, though, one of the most memorable hiring interviews was when my phone rang at work, the receptionist telling me in a shaking voice that some people in uniforms were there to see me. As I left my room to greet these guests, I saw four guys. They were standing straight and stiff, as if at attention. I tried to understand their rank and what did they want from me. I invited the gentlemen to my room, and we chatted for more than an hour. As we made small talk, I was still trying to understand what the hell was going on. Finally, one of the guys opened up, saying that he had seen a job advertisement from the company I was running, and wanted to personally deliver the résumé of their general's wife to me for the advertised role. I was stunned and quickly said we would consider her for the position, to end the conversation. I did end up interviewing and hiring her for the role. While I have no regrets and am happy to report that she performed entirely up to my expectations, I still believe I would not have hired her without the spectacular way her résumé was brought to me.

Before we finish the first chapter, let me remind you of a simple but constantly overlooked fact. Companies are institutions of profit. Shareholders in-vest to make money. They hire C.E.O.s to generate profits. C.E.O.s hire staff to help them realize this. To make money, each team member should not only compensate for their wages - usually much more than your 'take home,' due to taxes, social security, and benefits, but also create value to cover other expenses and capital investments the company has made since its inception, amortized to your tenure. If you can manage to create such value, you would be just about covering your cost to the company! Do not forget, the company expects profit!

In this respect, your value to the company should exceed or at least reach a minimum of ten times your cost to the company. This value depends on the actual amount of profit you generate or the perceived value you create or help create for your "sponsors" in the company, often the managers who hired you in the first place. In my experience, if this math does not add up for a sustained period, your job will not be secure in the long term.

MAKE AN AWESOME ENTRY!

Once the interview process is successfully completed, you will be offered a job. The entry starts at that stage, long before you physically enter the company's office!

Read your offer carefully. What does it say? Does it hold ambiguous promises that cannot be backed by contractual clauses? How do you clear them before signing the offer without upsetting the person offering you the job? It is wise to remember that you are at your strongest position to negotiate your employment conditions. Once you sign that offer and begin your post, it might be months or even years before some of those conditions change for the better.

I remember this one time when I was hired for a position overseas with a lucrative contract. As a part of the transition process, I resigned from my job, moved to this new country, and started work in my new role. A few days after I had settled in, I was informed that to be officially assigned to the position, I would need to pass an exam organized by the regulator in the local language. When I asked human resources, what would happen if I did not pass the exam, the person replied only half-jokingly that I would obviously be sent back "home."

Another time, I was in the process of being hired for a position. At the last minute, the employer put in front of me a contract that included specific clauses assigning all the responsibility for the damages related to the company to me, personally. This "All Inclusive Liability Contract" basically said that I would need to pay personally even if the office's windows broke. I negotiated the related clauses to a more acceptable format, limiting the liability amount to a percentage of what I would earn from my role in the company.

Both cases are relevant examples to show you that

before moving on to your new company, make sure you go through not the job offer but all contracts that you are supposed to sign. Because once you leave your current job, you are in, what I call, the "ambiguity period." Your new employer is aware of this and may well be capable of exploiting this time. Ask several times if needed, to make sure you see all the contracts you need to sign before resigning from your current role.

The best way to resolve the ambiguities at this stage is to find someone you trust in the company to discuss. For the sake of an example, let us say that the company offers you a company car, and you would like it to be a particular brand but are hesitant to ask human resources. Would you be able to ask this person you trust?

This person of trust could be any or friends of friends in that company. It could be easy to ask them the simple questions about the job conditions, but be careful not to reveal your job offer in full detail as an information leak could prove ugly for your fledgling career!

Another way to clarify these points is to talk to

the junior human resources staff member who is as-signed to complete your paperwork after accepting the job offer. You can always casually ask something like, "Hey, I did not want to ask the H.R. Director or the C.E.O. since I did not want to sound inappro-priate, but how much gas allowance are sales man-agers allowed?" Usually, they are happy to provide you with this information and also throw in some advice.

Get clarification on the terms and conditions of the job using all available sources. For information that requires an advanced explanation like stock options, long term incentives, etc. it is advisable to discuss this directly with the head of human re-sources as junior staff may not be informed about such compensation dynamics.

During this process, one thing usually overlooked is to discuss your targets for the year and the re-sources you would need to achieve those targets. It might not be realistically possible for you to dis-cuss this in detail at the current stage. However, any clarity you gain will be to your benefit once you start the job.

There could be cases where you would like to change certain parts of the offer. I have only one recommendation for you at this stage. Be prepared to hear 'no' as an answer and plan for it. Be selective in the negotiations you enter- a single 'no' is okay. Still, if you get rejected multiple times, this does not bode well for your position.

Finally, do not forget that the job offer is just the offer, a piece of paper. The job contract is what is supposed to secure your rights. Usually, one signs a job contract without giving them enough attention. We all tend to assume that job contracts accurately reflect what is in the job offer. To my experience, this is often not the case. While the discrepancies are mostly manageable, there is a small risk that a dispute may arise from a potential difference in the job offer and contact. Preferably you should ask for the job contract and have it checked out by a lawyer before you sign off the job offer. Once you sign the papers, do not forget to collect your signed copy.

You are all set and good to go! Good luck with your new job. Now, let us get you to make an impressive entry.

When you are making your physical entry into your new company, you should be careful of a few things. Even though the companies promote concepts like "change", "innovation", "collaboration", etc. most of them are, in fact, fiefdoms of power with syco-phants surrounding the decision-makers. As a naive fly wandering around the web with many spiders, if you do not watch out for these people, you can handicap yourself at the very beginning.

So, there lies the surprise, the most impressive entry is one made subtlety. Your entry should not be a big deal. At least you do not make it one.

When entering the company, your target is to be highly perceptive of the power structure and en-code it as much as possible. Your position's relative power will depend on your grade and the risks you are willing to take.

Every company has people who have been there for an exceptionally long time, and continue to work there, despite constant complaining. So, if you are only after a paycheck to feed your family, position yourself as a non-target, a low-risk person in the company relative to the power structure.

The people who approach you when you first arrive will be mostly pleasant and friendly. Yet, it is also true that some will want to assess how much of a risk you would create for them. How much will you challenge their current status quo? How likely are you to create extra work for them? Are you a challenge to their position? Can they use you in any way for their gain?

A few years ago, on an overseas assignment, a senior executive approached me from the company. We were from the same country of origin, and he told me that he would like to help me get oriented to the new company and the country. A year on, I realized that all his advice was utterly misleading, and he was only trying to exploit my position of power to his advance. I watched him use the same trick on all new hires from my country, using them with his perceived power in the company until they woke up and realized that the favors they were doing to him were not reciprocal. On the contrary, this gentleman was actively undermining them when interests clashed.

Of course, there will be predators who approach you in the guise of wanting to be friends. They prey on the relative naivety of a newcomer and try to work their agenda before the newcomer understands the company. The best way to dodge predators is to assess subtle cues they give off. Their reputation usually precedes them. Asking open-ended, non-binding questions to several colleagues, such as "What are the things that I should be careful about in the office?" will usually point you in the direction you should avoid.

The best way to avoid predators is to keep a safe distance from them. Having said that, predators, given their characteristics, usually wield a certain amount of power within the company. It may not be possible for you to avoid them. Take a cue from diplomats- develop your skills to engage predators in a basic conversation with minimal damage. At times, you might be willing to suffer some sort of damage to gain an advantage. This is a highly personal choice. One word of caution: predators never stop. Once you give, you will be asked to again and for more. So be careful where you start and where you stop.

The internet says that you can go to human resources to complain. Still, predators are predators
because they understand and control structures
within the company. Invoking company complaint
procedure is an intense process. Once you officially
make a complaint, you will be asked to provide
evidence. The evidence collection methods will be
contested. The evidence itself will be challenged.
Predators could deliberately make the process public to cause you emotional duress and unwanted
publicity.

Be careful of the cost of dealing with predators.

You may have heard about the tragic suicides of
the Chief Executive and C.F.O. of a leading global
insurer. These deaths are a sad example of how extremely toxic, micro, and open aggression in the
company and constant harassments can take you
down to your grave. Yes, it can get as dangerous as
this.

On a separate example, a famous Swiss investment
bank having its senior executives followed up by
detectives was important news. It is striking how

these companies promote workplace wellbeing while these horrific events continue to take place. Harassment by authority knows no boundaries if left unchecked.

I believe employers would be better off if they create systems and controls to capture and investigate harassment incidents rather than loudly announcing that their company is inclusive, fair, just, etc. It would be more credible to say that the company does the right thing when wrong things happen rather than P.R. bombing how inclusive the company is. If the private sector does not appropriately fulfill this mission, the government should step in and create a structure to investigate workplace issues independently. Companies should be publicly ranked according to their workplace wellbeing scores.

If you choose to fight the injustice or inappropriate behavior in your company, I would like to congratulate you on your courage. You should note that this will be a costly war for you. You are significantly decreasing your future employment prospects. In many countries, the human resources department of a company keeps track of blacklisted employees. They never get hired because of their prior publicity in office disputes.

Nevertheless, if you are convinced to fight this battle, make sure you have sufficient finances to sustain yourself. Ensure all the evidence you collect is valid, evidence that will withstand the scrutiny of a formal, legal court. For example, your record of text messages on your work phone may be sufficient for internal company processes. Still, it could be inadmissible if it proceeds to court.

If your complaint is resolved within the company and does not need to proceed to the court, be aware that your standing within the company, especially vis-à-vis your managers, will be different. It would help if you gave yourself some time to heal and then move on to another company after the dust settles.

Do not forget that whatever you share on social media will remain there and create negative publicity for you during the complaint resolution process. I would advise you not to share anything on social media unless you want to burn all bridges with future employment prospects.

KNOW YOUR BOUNDARIES

The company is a jungle made up of different spaces. Comparable to the Paleolithic times, or the lives of early humans, each staff has already defined his/her area. As a new entrant, you should be careful not to trespass on someone else's space.

Here are some common trespassing mistakes.

Engaging With Someone Else's Staff and Becoming Friends

Believe it or not, some people do not like their peers to become friendly with his/her staff. That is still a phenomenon that I hardly can believe, but I have seen it very often, it is something to watch for.

Speaking Up When Someone Else Was Supposed To

That is a big one. I have seen this in many companies, and the similarity across cultures still strikes
me to this day. People do have egos some beyond
primary control. A straightforward way to demon-
strate the ego is to speak up in meetings. There are
ideas, concepts, and domains owned by specific in-
dividuals. These concepts are mostly related to the
person's job description, but it can be slightly larger
than. It would be a costly mistake to trespass his/
her domain.

For example, let us say you are hired for an en-
gineering position. In a meeting, you wanted to
comment on the marketing campaign you happen
to have ideas and insights about. Be careful, this is
not your domain. Your comment will be heard and
understood, probably as a direct assault on the marketing person's competence. How dare you make a
comment as such? Do you believe you possess more
experience, know-how than that person? Who are
you? Why now? All these questions run through the
mind of the marketing person, and as you can see,
these questions could be easily perceived as a direct

threat.

As in international relations, direct threats usually provoke a response. If the person who is going to respond to you is more powerful than you, it could cause irreparable harm. Unfortunately, there are still so few managers and executives who can take constructive feedback. Most people only want to hear approval and praise, especially in front of their colleagues and peers.

Assuming or Volunteering for an Assignment in Someone Else's Scope

This is an interesting one. You could be asked by a superior to take on a task that falls in someone else's domain. Very tricky! The manager may think that you could do the job better than the actual owner of the job. This may not be true, but it is precisely how it will be perceived as.

Suppose you mess up any aspect of the project. In that case, the person initially responsible could argue later that he/she could have done it much better had you not intervened! They could also make life difficult for you by harassing you verbally in meetings with words like "Thanks Susan, for participating in the project. We have done all the work so far, and now you arrive and share the success with us!".

Hence, it is a very delicate communication with that person and the manager to set the expectations and protocols in advance so that you come out of this unharmed.

Embarrassing Your Boss

This is a big one, and I am shocked to see how often it occurs. This is a basic rule; avoid embarrassing the very person who pays your salary. You can corner him/her in private - and that is sometimes asked for especially for higher positions as they do not want a yes man/woman - but never, ever embarrass your boss in public.

It sounds astonishingly simple, but this embarrassment can take multiple forms in each situation. You could say something directly contrasting your boss, or you could argue with them in public. You could choose to publicly disobey their orders and make light of their comments. You could mimic them in an unflattering way or go to lunch with their biggest competitor (inside the company with an opponent or outside the company with a commercial competitor), or even make a public statement beyond your scope. How about silly things like posing awkwardly in a group photo? All these are valid examples and do not forget, if you embarrass them, there is a remarkably high chance that it will bite you.

I know of a senior director who received public praise from a top government official for a project that the company had recently finished. The Chairman of the company was furious because he thought that it should have been him being praised. The senior director was psychologically abused for several months. When I last saw him, he was a shell of the man I knew, a walking ghost. He left the company shortly afterward.

Early in my career, I was working in the Middle East as a management consultant. I was friends with a delightful gentleman whose hobby was to share inspirational quotes with the entire company via email. Please note that this was the early 2000s; social media was not as pervasive as today. One day he shared the following quote, "If life gives you lemons, put it in a shot of tequila and enjoy!" The problem was that there was a blanket ban on alcohol in that country. The C.E.O. immediately called him and questioned him harshly. The employee confessed he did not know what Tequila is. (I still doubt it to this day- I am sure he did not drink but he definitely knew). I followed him later to see he retired shortly after that. Forcing retirement was the only way to terminate people in the country.

Using Your Colleague's Property Without Their Permission

This could sound like a trivial matter, but it could go very far in making or breaking your impression amongst your co-workers. Be careful not to use other people's desks, computers, phones, mugs, etc. It could be used to paint you as inconsiderate and embarrass you in front of others. Be thoughtful before you use another person's belongings and always ask them for their permission.

The most common example is to park in someone else's place in the parking lot of the company. I did it once and take it from me, I will never do it again.

The organization's head of admin called me in a sheer panic and told me to immediately remove my car. I asked what the big deal was. He replied in utter terror that I had mistakenly parked in the spot of the owner's young and ambitious son. The guy was extremely sensitive about such a protocol. He told me that I should immediately remove my car before the egotistical son perceived it as an act of aggression.

The same company also had the protocol of parking cars with the back taillights facing the wall. The company owner did not want to see the back of a vehicle facing him as he entered the company. Hence, he drafted a policy where everyone was to park their cars with the headlights facing him when he came to the office parking lot.

This probably sounds like extreme examples to you, but I can say that I have seen such cases in local, multinational, and family-owned companies. I can assure you that taking care of these small nuances is crucial for your career and reputation.

DO YOU THINK YOU CAN EXIST WITHOUT A FIGHT?

There is zero chance that you will not be engaged in a 'fight' sometime in your professional career. I do not mean here the physical fistfight but rather a heated verbal confrontation. No matter what you do to avoid it, conflict is inevitable in a workspace.

Several years ago, I had a long, drawn-out argument with one of my peers. We could not agree on anything, and to be honest, everything she did felt like she was trying to undermine me. Not necessarily a result of our fight, but we both left the company later and moved on with our careers elsewhere.

Today, we are neighbors in the same community, and our kids play at the same playground. I meet her regularly while I am walking my dog, and we chat quite pleasantly. Amazingly, I remember how I was consumed day in day out with this at one point, and now there is no trace of the antagonism. To be truthful, I cannot even remember why we had those disagreements.

This is the big message of this chapter. You will forget your fights in the workplace. Make sure that you do not cause long-term harm to your standing in the company and career prospects when you start or continue them.

Keep in mind that there are two essential rules about fights:

Do not make it personal, and do not extend the conflict beyond a single conversation.

Everyone appreciates a person taking a stand and fighting for what he or she believes in. However, no one likes them when they become unreasonable and, thereby, contaminate the work environment's mental ecosystem. As a junior staff member, many young employees cannot distinguish between the dispute and the person they disagree with. This is such a fundamental difference yet so overlooked.

The dispute is the issue of conflict, the difference of perspective, or interpretations of facts differently by two or more people. It turns into a personal problem when either side or both sides get angry and start attacking another person's persona.

If you can differentiate between the dispute and person, you will be better positioned to handle conflicts at the workplace. It is easily said but difficult to execute, especially in the heat of the moment. The key to remaining calm and mature is to separate the dispute subject and the object of your brain's interpretation and associated story of your counterpart.

Calm your brain down and shut down this negative narrative in your mind about the person in front of you. This is how you will successfully handle the issue. Remember the story with my neighbor. We are figuratively at each other throats, several years ago, and now we walk my dog together.

In any conflict, you must assess who is 'attacking'

you. If you are the person disputing something and manage to remain calm, you control the situation. If you cannot stay unruffled, then you should teach yourself to stay composed. A wise man said once that "If you get angry, you lose".

If you are the one who is being attacked, it is a more delicate situation. If you run away from the fight, you will be perceived as a coward. The attacker could become a bully and benefit from your weakness going forward. If you allow such a relationship, it could, unfortunately, become socially acceptable as well, becoming the norm in dealing with you. Therefore, it is especially important to break the cycle even before it is conceived.

The advice is the same: try to remain as calm as possible, keep the discussion to the subject, be assertive in rejecting personal attacks by communicating how it is not appropriate for the workplace and your professional relationship.

I have always maintained that the best fight is the one that you do not need to get into. In fact, if you could manage to avoid active conflicts and try to find ways to solve them without tensions building, more productive discussions could be had. Sometimes, just giving situations a little bit of time and space helps sort things out.

To summarize, if you are working in an environment where teamwork, collaboration, and constructive criticism are appreciated (and I must say in most companies today, these are core values), then you should definitely follow this strategy. Become like water, fluid, and flexible, no matter what the situation may be.

COMMON TRAPS

When you work for a company, there are a few things that you should be incredibly careful of. These things do not look particularly dangerous at first but could sometimes cause huge issues if ignored.

One of these things is employee satisfaction surveys. These surveys are done to assess the state of the employee's professional wellbeing. However, the problem arises from the alternate courses of action the company takes to solve the issues that arise from the survey.

The first method is to dig deeper into the issues that come to light and understand the core problems raised and bring about constructive solutions. Unfortunately, this is what only 0.1% of the organizations do. The other 99.9% do it to understand any occurring mismanagement so that they can hold the managers responsible and replace incompetent ones with capable leaders.

As this is common knowledge, in the end, these managers start punishing their subordinate employees, since they take the results of low satisfaction scores personally.

The punishment could come in different ways. I do not necessarily mean that the employees receive direct harsh treatment from the managers. This is forbidden in most multinational companies but might happen in smaller or private organizations.

Mistreatment can come in different indirect forms. One such way is to add additional workload on the employees in the guise of 'initiatives.' What happens if you assign someone additional workload on top of that someone's regular workloads to improve the employee satisfaction score? The answer is this is perceived as a punishment, and the managers start doing everything. They can increase the scores so that they do not receive this sort of punishment anymore.

In the end, it is the employee who suffers. Be careful and assess whether the organization is committed to taking meaningful action and bringing about substantial change through the survey results. If this is not the case, be prepared to have your input in the survey used against you.

You could be part of a punishment circle without your consent. You could find yourself a group trying to find solutions to the problems you have highlighted yourself. This is not so bad if it is in your capacity to solve the issue raised. However, people usually raise questions in these surveys for top management to consider and change course. But in the end, it usually bounces back to those who raised the issue, who lack sufficient power in the organization to solve it. In the end, the purpose is not to change but to silence those who complain.

It is also imperative to point out that no survey is anonymous, as someone always knows who you are. It is up to that someone to conceal or reveal the data to the company's human resources. Be especially careful of the comments you provide in the survey. They may disclose your identity even if the study is conducted anonymously.

No institution audits the providers of these employee satisfaction surveys. I would be extremely interested to see a detailed external audit result of these institutions' practices, especially data privacy. If such audits are done, we will gain complicated insights into whether these surveys work for or against employees in general.

Another area where I would advise you to be cautious is the company's professional self-development training. In this training, you are asked to provide a lot of personal information. Some of this information could be sensitive, and it could reveal your weaknesses or shortcomings. You could be providing this information with an intent to benefit from the training. However, these trainers are often 'in the league' with the human resources department. They have more than one purpose when they provide the training. The so-called confidentiality statements such as "what we talk here will stay in this room" and claims of "this is a safe space" are simply untrue. Be incredibly careful in what data you provide and try not to reveal anything that could be used against you in performance reviews or any decisions to do with career progression.

Another overlooked ploy in the corporate world is the 'office party'. In every official celebratory gathering, there are drinks and food, often provided on the house. There is an immense temptation to overindulge. However, alcohol loosens your inhibitions. Keep your consumption to a minimum. A quick trick is to know your intake limit, divide your limit by two, and drink half as much. There will be one or two parties in your company every year. Still, there are approximately 200 other days to see your colleagues at work.

If you do not want to be the office clown, watch for what and how much you consume at the party. Leave early. If you are going to binge drink and get wasted, go out with your friends, switch off your iPhones, and do as you please. Your friends will not publicly embarrass and humiliate you with your previous night's antics, but your co-workers probably will. That is why they are called co-workers, not friends.

Another situation where you should have your

guard up is at meetings. As a newcomer, you should be mindful of the power dynamics in such spaces. It would be wise to remember that your office is not a democracy. Here, autocracy with a strict hierarchy prevails. I have seen the management system of some companies that could easily be classified as pure fascism if social scientists were to examine them.

Fascism is a form of government (or management) defined by authoritarian ("I am the boss, do as I say") and dictatorial power (power in the hands of the few such as Board and C.E.O.). It is recognized by the forcible suppression of opposition (try criticizing the C.E.O. in the town hall or company intranet to see what I mean) and strong regimentation of society (strict rules of conduct for the workforce). Sound familiar?

When you look at governance methods from democracy to monarchy, and towards dictatorship and fascism, no government in the world is proud to be classified as a fascist dictatorship. But very contrary to countries, corporate companies are pleased to be classified as such. The only trick is that they do not call it fascist dictatorship but conveniently name this "Corporate Governance".

For example, many famous multinational companies have operations worldwide, who never have
non-native C.E.O.s or top management team mem-
bers.

Companies are proudly run in a way that is sym-
bolic of a fascist dictatorship but with more beautiful labels for their policies. This strict form of
governance usually starts from the C.E.O. and ends
at the janitor. Everyone has a place in the organization, and the power dynamics can be complicated.

While taking part in meetings, do not take what
you have been asked literally. Your manager might
ask you a rhetorical question that does not call for
an answer or your opinion but instead, for a con-
firmation of his view. If you can distinguish between these nuances, your career will flourish, and
you will thrive instead of merely surviving.

When you have the chance to voice your opinions,
try to understand what is expected of you at that
time and place. Unfortunately, in a lot of organizations, when you have the opportunity to speak up,

it is not your opinion that is asked for. What is expected is your compliance and approval. If you choose to rebel and be an idealist, as I did in the early stages of my career, you have decided to go down a risky path.

On a rare occasion, being yourself and speaking up regularly could enable a career breakthrough. This is especially true if the people in power are asking for change. However, most organizations are happy as they are, and they expect you to maintain the status quo.

I do not want to sound negative here, but this is what I have experienced in the last 20 years working for many different companies in different positions.

In my experience, the only way you could speak up and voice your opinions while disregarding the power structure is in the exceptional case of an organization undergoing radical change and experiencing a power vacuum. This vacuum creates career opportunities, and if you go down this path, you might well be rewarded. In all other cases, you are expected to be compliant, obedient, and supportive.

Alternatively, suppose you have a position of power in the company (say you are a critical I.T. infrastructure manager in the company) or are independent (maybe you are not on the payroll but work as an agent for the company). In that case, you can indeed use your position to advance your points more forcefully. There might be consequences, but you can weather them with your position of strength.

In instances where there is a need to highlight something important to the management, I recommend making it in a private environment. Never do it publicly. Before you give this feedback, be attentive to the mood of the person in front of you. Withdraw your criticism if you encounter strong resistance or non-acceptance.

You are not the savior of the company. You are a paid employee on a contract, temporary or permanent, which also includes termination clauses. Do not get ahead of yourself and try to be a messiah. In a professional environment such as a typical corporate set up, it is the man against man. Put your interests before those of your co-workers. The cold, bitter truth is that if you find yourself out in the cold someday, none will shield you.

WINTER IS COMING

At some point, you might conclude that your services are no longer required in the organization or that you do not want to work there anymore. That is the point when the "divorce" begins between the company and you.

It might also happen that the company decides that your services are expendable. Before the company proceeds to terminate your employment, you should open your eyes to the preliminary signs. These large and small signals give you clues as to the current 'mood' of the organization. Sometimes the signals could be big ones such as recent changes in the top management and the undergoing of a significant restructuring due to pressure from shareholders or regulators. These conditions are ripe for change. Often, quick decisions are taken to achieve results that are perceived to be crucial for the company's viability or continued success.

Influential leaders take pride in making bold decisions, regardless of consequences. The idea here is to act first, see the results later, and adjust accordingly. As Nietzsche once said, "What does not kill me makes me stronger". To reach immediate results, upper management will take robust actions. Herein lie both your opportunity and danger.

The opportunities arise as people leave the organization creating a need for collaborators to implement the top management's agenda. If you can position yourself in line with their strategy, it could open new avenues of opportunity.

On the other end, if you are a vulnerable position, perhaps having suffered a recent low-performance rating or poor communication with the people in power, you might just find yourself without a job.

In such perilous conditions, what you can do is be compliant with the company's agenda and not exhibit any resistance. In anxious times such as these, if you ever show opposition to the change agenda, your head will roll amazingly fast. You will be re-placed just as quickly as you were fired.

At the risk of sounding like a stuck record, you should always remind yourself that companies are not democracies. Corporate structures are often like the Roman Armies of 500 BC- extremely au-thoritarian. Instead, this structure does not like criticism and requires people to get in line with a pre-decided vision.

This is especially evident at times of radical change. Those who speak up against change at these times are the ones who live the shortest. Be especially cautious at company surveys and meetings where you are encouraged to stand up and speak your mind. These are tricks to spot rebellious employ-ees. Do not be fooled! Corporate history is chockfull of people who speak up at the wrong time and get the sack.

Instead of resisting change, focus on looking for your next job.

The optimal time to leave your current job is when

you can find a better one. Your chances of finding a new job when you are unemployed will be significantly lower, it is just Murphy's law. Anything that can go wrong will.

Suppose the human resources team learns that you are looking for a job. In that case, you can logically explain that you are feeling anxious and insecure because of the fast-paced changes currently occurring in the organization. This is why you were looking for other options- a perfectly understandable explanation.

In fact, this reasoning could even persuade the human resources to offer you additional incentives to stay on if your value is perceived as crucial. Grab the opportunity with both hands.

It is crucial to have a cool head during these turbulent times. Everyone is under stress, and you not adding to this pile of this is very valuable. Your cool head also projects your self-confidence, which in turn opens new doors for you. Keeping your cool is the most trusted identifier of your professional and mental competency.

A few years ago, I found myself in the middle of a merger of two identical banks. Understandably, everyone was concerned because, for every available role, two candidates existed. Looking back, without exception, those candidates who held their cool, networked behind the doors and kept their team together survived termination, downgrades, or transfers and eliminated the ones who panicked or got frustrated. I remained calm and confident throughout and was rewarded with an upgraded position and a significant raise in salary. I would have never guessed that my career would advance as quickly. These times of turbulence and crises are, in fact, when the most significant opportunities arise.

One of my colleagues used to work for a company that went bankrupt due to fraud. Practically all the business magazines in the world wrote about it. Being a C.F.O. within the company in another unrelated country, he found his career stained. However, he was able to keep it together and navigate these waters so cleverly that he was promoted to Chairman & C.E.O. to help liquidate one of the entities while keeping his job as C.F.O. in another operation country. He ended up making 3x more money. While these new positions were not sustainable, he worked at those positions for a year, translating to three years in his previous post, financially speaking. I believe none of us can guarantee our places in this volatile world for three years, so he broke even from what I see. If life gives you lemons, you put it in Tequila and enjoy it!

SHOULD I STAY, OR SHOULD I GO?

To be fair, this decision is very personal, and no one else can take it on your behalf. However, let us consider several facts that might help you make this crucial decision.

A checklist of Pros and Cons of leaving your company may include the following points to consider:

(+) fresh new start (if you have issues with your current company)

(+) potentially higher salary, benefits, and position

(+) you can have a break or holiday between jobs (this is the best holiday to my experience as there is no outstanding jobs or assignments with the previous employer and the new one has not started yet)

(-) you need to develop your network in the new company from scratch, to get things done

(-) there is usually a trial period with the new company where your job is not secure (sometimes up to 6 months)

(-) the annual bonus could be paid pro-rata if you start in your new role in the middle of the year

(-) you may need to move to be closer to your new job

(-) if an economic crisis or financial problems are developing in the company and headcount rationalization occurs, usually a 'last come first out' principle will apply.

The most substantial salary increases you are going to get will be through job transfers. The single most common reason for this is that organizations do not increase an employee's salary significantly since it creates an unavoidable precedent. Suppose human resources give one employee a considerably significant wage increment. In that case, it will need to provide other high performing employees the same increase. This will not be a financially sustainable practice to adopt.

This is a universal phenomenon I have seen in large corporations and smaller public and private companies.

On the other hand, if someone is hired from another company, fewer people will question their compensation. There is no reliable benchmark as to how much remuneration they were receiving in their previous role.

This simple phenomenon is the most critical factor in determining the salary you secure and the chance to upgrade it.

Another factor to be considered is the sustainability of income. We have partly touched on the subject in the previous section. If the work environment is going through a complete upheaval, we should think about an effective change. At the same time, be careful to watch out for the signs that indicate the next company you are considering is also full of traps and pitfalls. Every job change is inherently risky; one of the significant risks being the mandatory trial period in which the employer could fire you with a minimal cost to the organization.

The other significant risk often shows up during the recruitment process when the new company does not reveal its real face. It shows its best self to lure you into the organization. This is, of course, a typical human trait. We show the best side of our personalities and put up a farce of excellence.

However, when you actually start work at said company, you can experience significant disappointment. The level of this disillusionment will depend on how much the company has 'tricked' you during the hiring process.

Hence, it is imperative to be mindful of these inherent impacts, even when deciding on an inevitable change.

The art of leaving a company is a delicate process. You must handle this gracefully because you never know when you might come across ex co-workers in different organizations. You might also need your H.R. and boss for future job references.

It is essential to manage your exit process diplomatically. Nobody wants to hear that you are leaving them for someone better. You must present a valid reason that will not antagonize them and convince them to let you go without creating a mess. Many organizations in the world delight in creating chaos if you try to leave in an unanticipated way. The problems they could generate for you include but are not limited to

(-)Delaying your exit using employer legal rights,

(-)Interfering in the recruitment process of your new employer, and

(-)Using contractual clauses to minimize your monetary benefits during the exit process.

Considering all these avoidable issues, it is in your best interest to manage this process with a delicate and diplomatic touch.

The exit is best discussed with the human resources or your manager directly, without disclosing it to your colleagues. You should only formally apply for resignation after you have had this conversation. Do not rush to send in your resignation letter. Suppose your boss and H.R. receive this resignation letter out of the blue, without proper dialogue. In that case, they might perceive it as a threat, and the risks outlined previously could materialize.

In discussion with your boss or human resources, show flexibility in your conduct and do your best to accommodate their modest requests. These requests could range from extending your exit process for several weeks to providing some support for a limited time after you leave the company or something as simple as keeping the resignation confidential.

Suppose you happen to be one of the company's extraordinarily talented employees. In that case, the boss and H.R. might well put out a counteroffer to stay in your current role. This is when it becomes a personal choice. I have seen people who have rejected a counteroffer and proceeded to leave the company without a problem. I have also seen people who have accepted a counteroffer and stayed.

There is the unlikely chance that you might have discovered something within the new company during your exit process that has discouraged you from switching to them. At that stage, a counter-offer from your current company would be a God-send for you. Unless this rare case sounds like your situation, I would not recommend accepting a counteroffer.

To be frank, accepting a counteroffer to stay in the present company often decreases your leverage. If you do indeed accept this counteroffer, it will be forgotten in three to four months. However, the person who proposed the counteroffer will always remember that you have increased his costs, a pun-ishment in the corporate world. He/She will be re-sentful for a long time because of that.

On the other hand, if you reject the counteroffer and leave the company as planned, it speaks volumes of your personality and commitment to your new em-ployer, especially if the counteroffer you received is better than what you are getting from the new com-pany. This would appear to be a very noble course of action and could be a sound basis for future wage negotiations in the new company.

As a summary, the pros and cons of staying in your current job after a counteroffer has been made are as follows:

(+) you will increase your current salary and get a promotion

(+) you show your employer that you are employable elsewhere

(+) your current job is secure for mid to long term

(+) if you play your hand right, your stay could be perceived as being loyal to the company

(-) if you play your hand badly, you will always be remembered by your boss for your disloyalty

(-) you might miss a bigger salary and a higher position

(-)potential personal reputation issues with headhunters and recruiters

TEARS DRY ON
THEIR OWN

The business world has seen many C.E.O.s, leaders, managers, consultants, and associates who have done more than their fair share and yet have faded away without leaving a legacy behind for the world to remember them.

In today's cut throat professional corporate culture, this is the inevitable fate of the modern white-collar slave. At the core of every business structure are shareholders who have chosen to invest in that company because they expected higher returns on their investments than other alternatives. In this equation, you are a cost. As you diminish in relative value, so will your employment conditions and remuneration. All the excellent work you have done is the property of the company you are working for;

praise and credit for your work will always be temporary.

It is up to you how you manage the process of separation from your existing company. You can choose to exit gracefully with a good reputation or watch the company terminate your employment.

Whichever hand you are dealt, play the short and long-term game. While this does not guarantee that you will be satisfied with the outcome, what it will bring is an assurance that you will make the most of the choices you are presented with.

This reminds me of a beautiful song by the late Amy Winehouse that goes, "Tears Dry on Their Own, " denoting that you will have to confront what's coming at some level. No matter how rough it gets, you know that things will turn out well.

It would be best if you prepared yourself for the inevitable end while you are still working. I have seen many C.E.O.s, owners, and directors who cannot let go of their work not because they need it financially, but because they set up their entire life around work. This is exceptionally shallow. While you are still working, you should parallelly think about an alternative stream of income for the period when you will not be actively employed. Additionally, you should be developing yourself towards this targeted activity while you are working. The notion that even if your current job does not exist, you will still have an income to sustain your life is very relieving.

But let us not just stop there, it is also vital to develop hobbies for your life. Five days with 7-8-hour days each or 40+ hours work life is a long time, and once it is gone, you might find yourself extremely bored. What will you do when you have this time free for yourself? I doubt many of us ask ourselves this question seriously. The cliché world tour or long holiday is just a one-off activity, and it is unlikely to keep you happy in the long term. In my blog at www.survivetheoffice.com, I share more on this topic and share good practices from around the world for you to consider.

The punchline is that you must plan for your financial future and mental happiness in the future while employed.

CONCLUSION

One way or another, it will all end- the fanfare, the
benefits, the paid vacations, company events, business class travel, the office perks...

You should actively start planning for the period
that follows. I urge you to start today. I see many
genuinely wonderful and smart people still naively
plowing away as if this will continue forever. Make
no mistake, it will not.

Yesterday, there were lifetime employment opportunities and state-sponsored employment with
health plans. Today, in the new world, our responsibility is to take care of our physical and mental
health and our finances. The idea that an office job
or more realistically, a succession of office jobs for
20 years will give you these guarantees is irrational.
You will not be worth a dime when the corporate

world does not need you anymore. This is not an anti-capitalism, rage-filled statement. It is the brutal truth.

Your life is more than your office or work. Your life is also more than the Friday night outs, weekends, and occasional holidays. Make it count. Make it mean something so that when someone remembers you tomorrow, they remember the person you were to them, rather than the tasks you did at work.

Ending this on a Maya Angelou quote is appropriate, considering the current state of the world – " I have learned that people will forget what you said, people will forget what you did, but people will never forget how you made them feel."

ACKNOWLEDGMENTS

I would like to thank all my bosses throughout these years for helping me finally to realize that all this corporate life is not what it initially seemed to be. I know they were not intentionally mean-spirited, but some were extremely narcissistic to the unfortunate detriment to their surroundings.

I also learned that the "values" voiced loudest in a company are the ones often missing.

I learned that when my bosses were tearing someone down, they were releasing pent-up anger at their own shortcomings.

Finally, I learned that the more we stay silent, the more we lose a part of ourselves.

This book is how I chose to express myself.

ABOUT THE AUTHOR

Jeremy Young

The author uses the pen name Jeremy Young to conceal his identity as he is still employed within a Fortune 500 company.

Throughout his 20 years' career, he has worked in many different countries for U.S., European, Asian companies including public, private, family-owned ones.

He has held many different roles, including C.E.O., board member, C.F.O., chief sales and marketing officer, and consultant.

He likes to spend his summers in the Mediterranean and travels a lot. He hopes a definite cure for COVID-19 is found as you read these lines so that the world can go back to normal, and he can resume his travels.

He dreams of buying a small boat with the proceeds of this book to sail the Mediterranean and live out his bucket list.

His website www.HowToSurviveTheOffice.com is intended to remind everyone of the indisputable facts of office life via real stories and allow everyone to share work and office stories anonymously as they wish. He will also contribute advice to your problems and maintain a platform where you can safely share your issues.

Many of us still trade our time for money. When you realize that your office is simply a place where this transaction occurs daily, you might be able to rid yourself of the undue pressure you put on yourself.

Please share your work and office stories on www.HowToSurviveTheOffice.com and keep the discussion going.

Printed in Great Britain
by Amazon

22780331R00047